This
Single
Thread

Paul Chambers

Paul Chambers (signature)

*A*lba Publishing

Published by Alba Publishing,
P O Box 266, Uxbridge
UB9 5NX, United Kingdom
www.albapublishing.com

A catalogue record for this book is available from the British Library

ISBN: 978-1-910185-25-4
Edited, designed and typeset by Kim Richardson
Cover photo © Kari Høglund/Dreamstime
Printed and bound by Bookpress.eu

10 9 8 7 6 5 4 3 2 1

Acknowledgements

The haiku in this collection have appeared previously in the following publications: journals *Acorn, A Hundred Gourds, Blithe Spirit, Bottlerockets, Cattails, Chrysanthemum, Frogpond, Heron's Nest, Mayfly, Modern Haiku, Presence, Shamrock, Snapshot Press, Wales Arts Review*, and *World Haiku Review*. Some of the haiku have also featured in US anthologies such as *Big Data*, (Red Moon Press, 2014), and *Haiku 2015* (Modern Haiku Press 2015). Some haiku have also appeared on the English language haiku websites of national Japanese newspapers, *Asahi Shimbun* and *Mainichi*.

haiku

early sun
the mist pulls away
from the river

ash on my sleeve
the first shades of dawn
over the docks

this single thread –
a spider crosses
the spring moon

first dusk stars
a gull's wing tips
holding light

sun in the ribs
of the old pier
ebb tide

through spring mists
the gulls on the bridge fall
one by one

a caterwaul
sets off the dogs
spring moon

evening wind
a feather trembles
in the grass

heat shimmer
the first blooming
railroad flowers

a wasp caught
in the net curtain
distant thunder

dust trembling
in the cobweb
spring night

fleeting wind –
the branch reaches after
the sparrow

morning haze
a lawnmower scatters
grass scent

driftwood –
boys stabbing
a jellyfish

moorland path
the sun mining
foxglove scent

mist burning back
a spider climbs inside
the sun

day moon
the potato seller asleep
in the grass

evening heat
my dog and I
share a yawn

JESUS
spelt out in rocks
desert roadside

cicada plainsong
the sun lingers in
the olive field

late afternoon
a boy leaps
my shadow

august night
the moon chooses us
to follow

pine trees
stripped by fire
yellow moth

pylon hum
the twitch of fibres
in a horse's shoulder

burnt out car
in the late sun
a gnat swarm

field of dead grass
a horse tethered too tight
to lie down

field of dead grass
the wind
loses its breath

summer dusk
girls chalk their shadows
on the new tar

sea at its far ebb
starfish left to dry out
in the sun

between the timbers
of the burnt house
summer moon

evening breeze
the sun clutching
thistle blooms

lilt of fishing boats
this quiet night
of quiet stars

a gull drifts
beyond the hill
summer deepens

through the eye
of the hare's skull
yellow grass

a donkey tethered
to a tractor tyre
dead sunflowers

dusk sun –
a gull pulls away
from its shadow

falling star
silence follows
silence

thinning moon
the screech of cicadas
in the railroad grass

darkening sky
beneath the pylon
horses tighten

magnolia scent
a night in september
no matter which

my shadow too
will be gone
moonless night

lying still
after making love
windblown leaves

distant gulls
the sand shifts over
the sand

autumn dusk
a cormorant sets down
on its shadow

woken by thirst
the rain against
my window

pale sun
maple branches reach
through yellow

overnight train
a coat sleeve swaying
from the luggage hold

pigeons mating
dark water trapped
in the grout lines

fierce autumn wind
the spider holds the crane fly
still

in the brown river
they search for a body
hammering rain

each leaf
the sparrow brushes
falling

lightning –
the spider slips deeper
into the bath

autumn wind
the sky on the water
broken

late morning –
rain in the hollow
of a punctured ball

after a storm
uncertain birds
uncertain river

autumn mist
a cat's eyes catch
the headlights

all morning
the rain plucking yellow
leaves

rail tunnel
the open mouth
of a fox carcass

clouds torn
the wind breaks
on the water

storm clearing
the leaves grow heavy
with stars

burnt autumn sky
the fold
of a shot deer

mist of my breath
a spider's web torn
in the kissing gate

empty sky
the dead child's clothes still
hanging on the line

winter crow
an eyelash
on your pillow

overnight train
a handprint smears
the moon

quieter now
than before it came
first snow

faint south wind
she catches the first snow
on her eyes

first snow falling
through old leaves
falling

sharing the bath
the rippling
of a dead star

a strand of her hair
clings to the soap –
midwinter cold

winter moon
downstream a duck breaks
from the water

rusted rail track
fading slowly
early snow

christmas morning
a sparrow breaks the crumbs
from the broken bread

faint morning breeze
the shifting light
of the cobwebs

red sky –
a ribbon of swallows
in the dead tree

mist on the window
her small hand
traces a prayer

winter stars
breadcrumbs
sinking

returning snow
the lines of your car
fading

morning moon
a glove on the railing
cradles the frost

the knife grinds
through a fish's stomach
winter deepens

collecting snow
the crane arm
hooked still

mists caught
in the nettle thicket
the cry of a lamb

refrigerator hum
my prayer
trails off

drizzling rain
my reflection
in the hearse

winter fields
the *caw* of a crow
breaks in the mist

dawn breaking
the thawing lamb
starts to bleed

white mist
the wing and the wave
almost touching